MILLIONAIRE PROPERTY MASTER CLASS

THE COMPLETE RENTAL PROPERTY COURSE: FROM FINDING TENANTS TO MAXIMIZING ROI

I0408895

REMI KUTI

Copyright © 2023 **Remi Kuti.**

All rights reserved. This book or any portion thereof may not be reproduced or used in any manner whatsoever without the express written permission of the publisher except for the use of brief quotations in a book review.

Table of Contents

Introduction

Overview of the book

The Complete Rental Property Course: From Finding Tenants to Maximizing ROI, is a comprehensive guide for property investors who want to achieve success in real estate investing. This book is designed to provide property investors with the knowledge and tools they need to succeed in the real estate market.

The book is divided into several chapters that cover different aspects of real estate investing. The first chapter provides an introduction to real estate investing and outlines the benefits of investing in rental properties. The subsequent chapters cover topics such as finding the right property, financing options, property management, tenant screening, lease agreements, marketing rental properties, and maximizing ROI.

The book is written in a clear and concise manner, making it easy for property investors of all levels to understand. It is packed with practical tips, real-world examples, and case studies that provide a comprehensive overview of real estate investing.

Whether you are a beginner or an experienced property investor, this book is an invaluable resource that will help you achieve your real estate investing goals. It provides a step-by-step guide that will help you build a successful real estate portfolio and maximize your returns.

The book is also suitable for individuals who are interested in pursuing a career in real estate investing. Real estate courses, property management courses, and real estate development courses can benefit from the comprehensive information provided in this book.

In summary, The Complete Rental Property Course: From Finding Tenants to Maximizing ROI is a must-read for property investors who want to succeed in the real estate market. It is a practical guide that will provide you with the knowledge and tools you need to build a successful real estate portfolio and maximize your returns.

Why rental property is a good investment

Rental property is one of the most lucrative investments you can make. It offers numerous benefits that make it a great investment option for property investors. In this subchapter, we will discuss why rental property is a good investment and how it can help you maximize your ROI.

Firstly, rental property provides a steady stream of income. A rental property generates income through rental payments made by tenants. This income can be used to repay the mortgage, pay for property taxes, maintenance costs, and other expenses. With the right property management, rental income can provide a stable and reliable source of income for years to come.

Secondly, rental property appreciates over time. Real estate is a tangible asset that, historically, has appreciated in value over time. While there may be fluctuations in the market, real estate has always been a sound investment. As the property appreciates, the investor's equity in the property increases, providing a larger return on investment.

Thirdly, rental property provides tax benefits. Rental property investors are eligible for a number of tax deductions, including mortgage interest, property taxes, insurance, and repairs and maintenance costs. These deductions can offset rental income, reducing your taxable income and lowering your overall tax burden.

Fourthly, rental property offers diversification. Investing in rental property is a great way to diversify your investment portfolio. Unlike stocks and bonds, rental property is a tangible asset that can provide a consistent income stream and long-term appreciation.

Lastly, rental property allows for greater control. As a rental property owner, you have control over the property, including the ability to make renovations and upgrades. This control allows you to increase the property's value and rental income, maximizing your ROI.

n conclusion, rental property is a great investment option for property investors. It provides a steady stream of income, appreciates over time, offers tax benefits, diversifies your portfolio, and allows for greater control. As you begin your journey in rental property investing, it is important to equip yourself with the right knowledge and skills through a property course, real estate investing course, property management course, rental property course, commercial property course, residential property course, real estate development course, vacation rental course, short- term rental course, real estate flipping course, or luxury property course. With the right education and guidance, you can maximize your ROI and achieve financial success through rental property investing.

Who this book is for

The Complete Rental Property Course is a comprehensive guide that is designed for property investors who are looking to maximize their rental property profits. Whether you are a seasoned real estate investor or just starting out, this book provides you with the knowledge and tools you need to succeed in the rental property market.

If you are planning to invest in rental properties, this book is for you. It is the perfect resource for individuals who are looking to build a profitable rental property portfolio, and want to learn how to find, purchase, manage, and maintain their properties to maximize their ROI.

This book is also ideal for property courses, real estate investing courses, property management courses, rental property courses, commercial property courses, residential property courses, real estate development courses, vacation rental courses, short-term rental courses, real estate flipping courses, and luxury property courses. It is designed to provide a comprehensive overview of the rental property market, and covers all aspects of real estate investing, from finding the right property to managing and maintaining it.

If you are interested in real estate investing, this book is a must-read. It provides you with the knowledge and tools you need to succeed in the rental property market, and helps you avoid the common pitfalls that many investors face. Whether you are looking to invest in residential or commercial properties, this book provides you with the information you need to make informed decisions and maximize your profits.

In short, this book is for anyone who is interested in real estate investing and wants to learn how to build a profitable rental property portfolio. It is an essential resource for property investors, property managers, real estate agents, and anyone else who is interested in the rental property market.

How to Use This Book:

The Complete Rental Property Course: From Finding Tenants to Maximizing ROI is a comprehensive guide for anyone interested in investing in rental properties. This book covers all aspects of rental property investing, from finding properties to managing them effectively. If you're a property investor looking to maximize your profits, this book is for you.

Here are some tips on how to use this book:

1. Start with the basics - If you're new to rental property investing, start with the basics. Read through the chapters on finding properties, financing, and evaluating potential investments. This will give you a solid foundation to build on.

2. Customize the content to your needs - This book covers a wide range of topics, from residential rentals to commercial properties. Choose the chapters that are most relevant to your specific needs and interests.

3. Take notes and make a plan - As you read through the book, take notes and start making a plan for your rental property investments. This could include identifying potential properties, creating a budget, and setting goals for your investments.

4. Use the worksheets and checklists - Throughout the book, you'll find worksheets and checklists that can help you stay organized and on track. Use these tools to keep track of your progress and make sure you're not missing any important steps.

5. Refer back to the book as needed - This book is designed to be a reference guide that you can refer back to as needed. Keep it on hand as you begin your rental property investing journey, and use it to troubleshoot problems and find new ideas for maximizing your ROI.

Overall, The Complete Rental Property Course is a valuable resource for anyone interested in rental property investing. Whether you're a seasoned investor or just starting out, this book will provide you with the tools and knowledge you need to succeed.

Finding the Right Property

Identifying the right neighborhood

Identifying the right neighborhood is a crucial step in real estate investing. The neighborhood you choose can make or break your investment. This is because the location of your rental property can affect the demand for it, the quality of tenants you attract, and the rental income you earn. Therefore, it is important to be strategic when selecting a neighborhood.

The first thing to consider when identifying the right neighborhood is the location. You want a neighborhood that is safe, accessible, and has a good reputation. Look for neighborhoods that are close to amenities such as schools, hospitals, shopping centers, and public transport. These amenities can attract tenants who are willing to pay a premium for convenience and accessibility.

Another factor to consider when selecting a neighborhood is the level of development. Look for neighborhoods that are undergoing revitalization, as these areas are likely to experience an increase in property value and demand. You can also consider neighborhoods that are in the path of progress, such as those that are close to major infrastructure projects like highways, airports, and train stations.

Furthermore, it is important to research the demographics of the neighborhood. Look for neighborhoods that have a high demand for rental properties. If you are targeting families, look for neighborhoods that have good schools and parks. On the other hand, if you are targeting young professionals, look for neighborhoods that have a thriving nightlife and entertainment scene.

You should also consider the competition in the neighborhood. Look for neighborhoods that have a high demand for rental properties but have a low supply. This can help you command higher rental income and attract quality tenants.

Lastly, consider the long-term prospects of the neighborhood. Look for neighborhoods that have a stable or growing population, as this is a good indicator of future demand for rental properties. Also, consider the potential for future development in the neighborhood.

In conclusion, identifying the right neighborhood is a crucial step in real estate investing. By considering factors such as location, level of development, demographics, competition, and long- term prospects, you can select a neighborhood that will maximize your rental income and ROI.

Assessing the Property Value

As a property investor, one of the most important things you need to consider is the value of the property you are considering investing in. The value of a property is not just about its price tag but also the potential for growth and return on investment (ROI) it offers.

To assess the value of a property, you need to consider several factors, including location, condition, size, and amenities.

Location is a crucial factor in determining the value of a property. Properties located in desirable neighborhoods with good schools, low crime rates, and access to public amenities like parks, shopping centers, and transportation tend to command higher prices. Properties located in areas with high crime rates, poor schools, and limited access to amenities are usually less valuable.

The condition of the property is also essential when assessing its value. Properties in good condition, with well-maintained structures and modern amenities, are more valuable than those in poor condition that require significant repairs or renovations.

The size of the property is another critical factor in determining its value. Larger properties with more square footage tend to be more valuable than smaller properties. However, the size of the property should be in line with the market demand in the area.

Amenities, such as swimming pools, gyms, and parking spaces, can also affect the value of a property. Properties with desirable amenities tend to be more valuable than those without them.

When assessing the value of a property, it's important to consider the potential for growth and ROI. Properties located in areas with a growing population and a strong economy tend to offer better growth potential. Properties with high rental income or potential for appreciation also offer better ROI.

In conclusion, assessing the value of a property is crucial to making informed investment decisions. By considering location, condition, size, amenities, and growth potential, you can determine the true value of a property and make a well-informed investment decision.

Analyzing the market

Analyzing the market is a crucial step in any rental property investment. Understanding the market trends, demands, and competition can help you make informed decisions and maximize your ROI.

To start analyzing the market, you need to conduct thorough research of the local real estate market. Look at the rental rates, vacancy rates, and the overall demand for rental properties in the area. You can use various online tools and websites to gather this information, such as Zillow, Redfin, and Rentometer.

Next, you need to consider the type of property you want to invest in. Are you interested in residential or commercial properties? Do you want to invest in vacation rentals or short-term rentals? Each type of property has its own market dynamics, so it's important to understand the specific market trends and demands for your chosen niche.

Another important factor to consider is the competition in the market. Look at the number of available rental properties in the area, their rental rates, and their amenities. This will give you an idea of what you're up against and help you determine how you can make your property stand out from the rest.

Additionally, you should consider the economic and demographic trends in the area. Look at the job market, population growth, and average income levels. These factors can have a significant impact on the demand for rental properties in the area and can help you make informed decisions about your investment.

Overall, analyzing the market is a critical step in rental property investment. By understanding the local market trends, demands, and competition, you can make informed decisions and maximize your ROI.

Property Inspection

One of the most important steps in the rental property process is property inspection. This step is critical to ensure that the property is in good condition and that any necessary repairs or maintenance are identified before renting to tenants. A thorough property inspection can also help protect the landlord from potential liability issues.

It is important to conduct a property inspection before purchasing any rental property. This will help identify any potential issues that may require repairs or renovations, and will also give the landlord an idea of what kind of ongoing maintenance will be required.

When conducting a property inspection, it is important to be thorough and to document any issues that are identified. This includes taking photographs and notes of any damage or wear and tear, as well as documenting any repairs that have been made.

It is also important to ensure that the property is up to code and meets all necessary safety requirements. This includes checking smoke detectors, carbon monoxide detectors, and fire extinguishers, as well as ensuring that any electrical, plumbing, or heating systems are in good working order.

If you are not familiar with property inspections, it may be worth hiring a professional inspector to conduct the inspection for you. This can help ensure that all potential issues are identified and that the property is in good condition before renting to tenants.

In addition to conducting a property inspection before renting to tenants, it is also important to conduct regular inspections throughout the tenancy. This can help identify any necessary repairs or maintenance that may need to be done, and can also help ensure that the tenants are taking care of the property.

Overall, property inspection is a critical step in the rental property process. By conducting thorough inspections before renting to tenants and throughout the tenancy, landlords can help ensure that their properties are in good condition and that any necessary repairs or maintenance are identified and addressed in a timely manner.

Financing options

Investing in rental property can be a great way to diversify your portfolio and generate passive income. However, financing this type of investment can be a challenge, especially if you don't have a lot of cash on hand. Fortunately, there are several financing options available to property investors.

One of the most common options is a traditional mortgage. This is a loan that is secured by the property you are purchasing. To qualify for a mortgage, you will need to have a good credit score, a steady income, and a down payment. The down payment requirement can vary depending on the lender and the type of property you are purchasing. Generally, you will need to put down at least 20% of the purchase price.

Another option is a home equity loan or line of credit. This is a loan that is secured by the equity in your existing home. If you have owned your home for a while and it has appreciated in value, you may be able to tap into this equity to fund your rental property purchase.

If you are purchasing a commercial property, you may be able to qualify for a commercial mortgage. This is a loan that is specifically designed for commercial properties, such as office buildings, retail spaces, and warehouses. Commercial mortgages typically have higher interest rates and stricter qualification requirements than residential mortgages.

If you don't have the cash or credit to qualify for a traditional loan, you may be able to find a private lender or hard money lender. These lenders are often willing to take on more risk than traditional lenders, but they also charge higher interest rates and fees.

No matter which financing option you choose, it's important to do your research and shop around for the best rates and terms. You should also have a solid understanding of the cash flow and potential ROI of your rental property investment to ensure that you can make your mortgage payments and generate a profit.

Preparing the Property for Rental

Property renovation

Property renovation is an important aspect of real estate investing, especially for rental properties. Renovating a property not only increases its value but also makes it more attractive to potential tenants. However, it is important to approach property renovation with caution and to have a well-planned strategy in place.

The first step in renovating a property is to assess its current condition and identify areas that need improvement. This can be done by conducting a thorough inspection of the property and making a list of necessary repairs and upgrades. It is important to prioritize repairs and upgrades that will provide the highest return on investment.

When renovating a rental property, it is important to keep in mind the target demographic of potential tenants. For example, if the property is located in an area with a high concentration of students, it may be more beneficial to focus on creating functional living spaces with plenty of storage rather than luxury finishes.

Renovation costs can quickly add up, so it is important to set a budget and stick to it. It may also be beneficial to work with a contractor or renovation team to ensure that the project stays on track and within budget.

When planning a property renovation, it is important to consider the timeline for completion. Renovations can disrupt the lives of tenants and potentially impact rental income, so it is important to plan ahead and communicate with tenants throughout the process.

In addition to increasing the value of a rental property, renovations can also improve the overall quality of life for tenants. By creating comfortable and modern living spaces, tenants are more likely to stay in the property long-term and provide a steady source of rental income.

Overall, property renovation is an important aspect of real estate investing and can provide a significant return on investment. By approaching renovations with a well-planned strategy and keeping the target demographic of potential tenants in mind, investors can create attractive and profitable rental properties.

Property staging

Property staging is a crucial aspect of any successful rental property business. It involves the art of presenting a property in the best possible light to potential tenants, with the aim of maximizing its potential and increasing its value. A well-staged property can attract more tenants, command higher rents, and ultimately increase your ROI.

The first step in property staging is decluttering and depersonalizing the space. This means removing any unnecessary items and personal belongings, such as family photos and personal décor. This allows potential tenants to visualize themselves in the space and creates a neutral canvas for staging.

The next step is to create an atmosphere that is both welcoming and functional. This can be achieved by using neutral colors, comfortable furniture, and tasteful décor. Lighting is also an important aspect of staging, as it can create a warm and inviting atmosphere.

Another important aspect of property staging is highlighting the property's best features. Whether it's a stunning view or a spacious living room, showcasing these features can help to attract potential tenants. This can be achieved through the use of strategically placed furniture and décor.

When it comes to staging, attention to detail is key. This includes everything from ensuring that the property is clean and well-maintained to making sure that all fixtures and appliances are in good working order. It's also important to consider the needs of your target market, whether it's families, young professionals, or retirees.

Overall, property staging is an essential part of any successful rental property business. By presenting your property in the best possible light, you can attract more tenants, increase your rental income, and ultimately maximize your ROI. Whether you're a seasoned property investor or just starting out, investing in property staging is a smart move that can pay off in the long run.

Property maintenance

Property maintenance is one of the most important aspects of owning a rental property. It's crucial to maintain the property in order to keep it in good condition and attract reliable tenants. Neglecting maintenance can result in costly repairs and a decrease in property value. In this subchapter, we'll discuss the key components of property maintenance and how to ensure that your investment is well-maintained.

The first step in property maintenance is to conduct regular inspections. Inspections allow you to identify any potential issues before they become major problems. During an inspection, you should check the property's exterior for any damage or signs of wear and tear. You should also inspect the interior of the property, including the plumbing, electrical system, and appliances.

Another important aspect of property maintenance is landscaping. A well-maintained landscape not only enhances the property's curb appeal but also helps to prevent damage to the property. Regularly trimming trees and bushes and removing dead or decaying plants can prevent damage to the property's foundation, roof, and walls.

In addition to regular inspections and landscaping, it's important to address any maintenance issues as soon as they arise. This includes repairing leaks, fixing broken appliances, and replacing damaged flooring or walls. Ignoring maintenance issues can lead to more expensive repairs down the line and can make it difficult to find and retain reliable tenants.

Finally, it's important to have a plan in place for emergencies. This may include having a list of reliable contractors or repair services on hand, as well as having a plan for addressing emergency repairs outside of regular business hours. Being prepared for emergencies can help to minimize damage to the property and ensure that tenants are safe and comfortable.

In conclusion, property maintenance is a critical aspect of owning a rental property. Regular inspections, landscaping, addressing maintenance issues promptly, and having a plan for emergencies are all key components of effective property maintenance. By taking a proactive approach to property maintenance, you can protect your investment and maximize your ROI.

Property insurance

Property insurance is an essential aspect of owning rental property. It protects your investment and provides peace of mind. Property insurance policies vary depending on the type of property, location, and risks involved. As a property investor, it is crucial to understand the different types of property insurance and how they can benefit you.

One of the most common types of property insurance is landlord insurance. This insurance covers rental properties and protects landlords from financial losses due to damage or loss of rental income. It also covers liability claims if a tenant or visitor is injured on the property.

Landlord insurance policies typically cover the structure of the building, personal property, loss of rental income, and liability.

Another type of property insurance is commercial property insurance. This insurance covers commercial properties such as retail stores, office buildings, and warehouses. Commercial property insurance protects against damage to the property, loss of income, and liability claims.

Residential property insurance is another type of property insurance that covers single-family homes, condos, and townhouses. This insurance covers the structure of the building, personal property, and liability. It also provides coverage for loss of use, which means that if a tenant is unable to live in the property due to damage, they will be reimbursed for living expenses.

Vacation rental insurance is another type of property insurance that is specifically designed for short-term rental properties. It covers the property, personal property, and liability. It also provides coverage for loss of rental income, which is essential for vacation rental properties that rely on seasonal income.

When choosing a property insurance policy, it is crucial to read the policy carefully and understand the coverage limits and deductibles. It is also important to shop around and compare policies from different insurance providers to ensure that you are getting the best coverage at the best price.

In conclusion, property insurance is an essential aspect of owning rental property. It protects your investment and provides peace of mind. As a property investor, it is crucial to understand the different types of property insurance and how they can benefit you. Make sure to choose a policy that provides adequate coverage and fits your budget.

Property taxes

Property taxes are an important consideration for any property investor. They are a recurring expense that must be paid annually and can significantly impact the return on investment (ROI) of a property. In this subchapter, we will discuss what property taxes are, how they are calculated, and strategies for managing them.

What are Property Taxes?

Property taxes are taxes levied on real estate by local governments. They are used to fund public services such as schools, roads, and emergency services. Property taxes are assessed based on the value of the property and are typically paid annually. The amount of property tax owed varies by location and can be a significant expense.

How are Property Taxes Calculated?

Property taxes are calculated by multiplying the assessed value of the property by the tax rate. The assessed value is determined by the local government and is based on the market value of the property. The tax rate is set by the local government and is expressed as a percentage of the assessed value. For example, if the assessed value of a property is $100,000 and the tax rate is 2%, the annual property tax owed would be $2,000.

Strategies for Managing Property Taxes

Property investors can use several strategies to manage property taxes and maximize ROI. One strategy is to appeal the assessed value of the property if it is higher than market value. This can be done by submitting a request for reassessment to the local government. Another strategy is to take advantage of tax exemptions and deductions. For example, some states offer tax exemptions for properties used for agricultural purposes or properties owned by veterans. Property investors can also deduct property taxes from their federal income taxes.

In conclusion, property taxes are an important consideration for any property investor. They are a recurring expense that can significantly impact ROI. Understanding how property taxes are calculated and implementing strategies for managing them can help property investors maximize their ROI and achieve their investment goals.

Finding and Screening Tenants

Advertising the Property

Advertising the property is crucial when it comes to finding potential tenants. The advertisement should be informative, appealing, and comprehensive. It should highlight the property's unique features, location, and amenities, among other things.

The first step in advertising the property is to determine the target audience. For instance, if the property is a luxury apartment, the target audience should be high-income earners. In contrast, if the property is a vacation rental, the target audience should be tourists. Once the target audience is established, the right advertising platforms can be selected.

The most common advertising platforms for rental properties include online classifieds, social media, and listing websites. Online classifieds such as Craigslist and Gumtree are popular because they are free and have a wide reach. Social media platforms like Facebook and Twitter are also ideal for advertising rental properties as they allow for targeted advertising. Listing websites like Zillow, Trulia, and Realtor.com are ideal for advertising properties to a larger audience.

When advertising a rental property, it is important to include high-quality photos and videos. This will give potential tenants an idea of what the property looks like and help them make an informed decision. The photos and videos should be taken during the day and should highlight the property's unique features.

In addition to photos and videos, the advertisement should also include a detailed description of the property. The description should highlight the property's key features, such as the number of bedrooms and bathrooms, the size of the property, and any unique amenities such as a pool or a balcony. The description should also include information on the property's location and nearby amenities such as schools, parks, and shopping centers.

Overall, advertising a rental property requires careful planning and execution. The advertisement should be informative, appealing, and comprehensive to attract the right tenants. By using the right advertising platforms and including high-quality photos and videos, property investors can maximize their ROI and find the right tenants for their rental property.

Tenant screening

Tenant screening is one of the most important aspects of being a successful rental property investor. It is a process that allows the landlord to evaluate potential tenants and determine if they are suitable for the property. The screening process is essential to ensure that the landlord can avoid any potential legal or financial issues that may arise from renting to the wrong tenant.

The first step in tenant screening is to create a rental application form that includes all the important information that a landlord requires from a tenant. This form should include personal details, employment status, rental history, credit score, and any relevant references. The application form is a crucial document that helps landlords to weed out unsuitable tenants before they even view the property.

Once an applicant has completed the application form, the landlord can then begin the screening process. This involves conducting a thorough background check, which includes checking the applicant's credit score, criminal history, and employment status. It is also important to verify the applicant's income and rental history.

One of the most effective ways to verify an applicant's rental history is to contact their previous landlords. This will allow the landlord to get a better understanding of the applicant's behavior as a tenant, such as paying rent on time, keeping the property clean, and respecting the property.

Another important aspect of tenant screening is to conduct an interview with the applicant. This is an opportunity for the landlord to get to know the applicant better and assess whether they are a good fit for the property. The interview should cover topics such as their lifestyle, interests, and any potential issues that may arise during the tenancy.

In conclusion, tenant screening is a crucial aspect of rental property investment that is often overlooked by landlords. By conducting a thorough screening process, landlords can avoid potential legal and financial issues and ensure that they have selected the right tenant for their property. Investing in a quality tenant screening process is a worthwhile investment that can lead to long-term success in the rental property market.

Lease agreements

Lease agreements are an essential component of the rental property business. A lease agreement is a legally binding contract between a landlord and a tenant that outlines the terms and conditions of the rental arrangement. It is important for both parties to understand the content of the lease agreement before signing it.

A well-drafted lease agreement is a critical component to a successful rental property investment. The lease agreement should clearly define the rights and responsibilities of both the landlord and the tenant and outline the terms of the lease. In order to ensure that the lease agreement is comprehensive and legally binding, it is recommended that landlords consult with an attorney or property management company.

A lease agreement should include the following information:

1. Names and addresses of both the landlord and tenant

2. The date the lease agreement begins and ends

3. The amount of rent and the due date

4. Security deposit requirements and conditions for its return

5. Pet policies, if applicable

6. Maintenance and repair responsibilities for both the landlord and tenant

7. Rules and regulations for use of the property

8. Procedures for resolving disputes and handling lease violations

9. Termination and renewal procedures

It is important for landlords to thoroughly review the lease agreement with the tenant before signing it. This provides an opportunity for any questions or concerns to be addressed and ensures that both parties fully understand the terms and conditions of the lease.

In conclusion, a well-drafted lease agreement is an essential component of a successful rental property investment. It is important for landlords to consult with an attorney or property management company to ensure that the lease agreement is comprehensive and legally binding. Thoroughly reviewing the lease agreement with the tenant before signing it is also critical to a successful rental arrangement.

Rent collection is an essential part of being a successful property investor. It is the primary source of income from your rental property, and it helps you keep your business running smoothly.

However, collecting rent can be a challenging task, especially if you don't have the right systems in place. In this subchapter, we will discuss the best practices for collecting rent and how you can streamline the process to maximize your ROI.

The first step in rent collection is setting up a system that works for both you and your tenants. This includes deciding on a due date for rent, providing multiple payment options, and outlining consequences for late payments. By setting clear expectations and guidelines, you can avoid misunderstandings and minimize the risk of payment delays.

One of the most effective ways to ensure timely rent payments is to use a property management software. With a good software, you can automate the rent collection process, send reminders to tenants, and track payment history. This will save you time and effort, and it will also provide you with an accurate record of rent payments.

Another important aspect of rent collection is following up with tenants who are late on payments. This can be a delicate situation, as you don't want to damage your relationship with your tenants, but you also need to enforce the terms of your lease agreement. It's best to approach the situation with empathy and offer solutions to help the tenant catch up on payments. This could include setting up a payment plan or offering a grace period for late fees.

Finally, it's essential to have a plan in place for dealing with tenants who consistently fail to pay rent. This may involve legal action, eviction, or even selling the property. It's important to consult with a legal professional and follow the proper procedures to protect your investment and your business.

In conclusion, rent collection is a crucial aspect of property investing, and it requires careful planning and execution. By setting up a system that works for both you and your tenants, using technology to streamline the process, and addressing payment issues with empathy and professionalism, you can maximize your ROI and ensure the success of your rental property business.

Tenant management

Tenant management is a crucial aspect of running a successful rental property business. As a property investor, it is important to ensure that your tenants are satisfied and that they are paying rent on time. In this subchapter, we will discuss the various aspects of tenant management and how to maximize your ROI.

The first step in tenant management is finding the right tenants for your property. This involves screening potential tenants to ensure that they have a good rental history and can afford the rent. You should also check their credit history and employment status to ensure that they have a stable source of income.

Once you have found the right tenants, it is important to maintain a good relationship with them. This involves responding to their concerns and complaints in a timely manner and ensuring that the property is well-maintained. Good communication is key to maintaining a good relationship with your tenants.

Another important aspect of tenant management is rent collection. You should have a clear rent collection policy in place and enforce it consistently. This includes sending out rent reminders and late payment notices, and taking legal action if necessary.

In addition to rent collection, you should also ensure that your tenants are aware of their responsibilities as tenants. This includes keeping the property clean and in good condition, and following any rules or regulations that you have set out.

Finally, it is important to keep track of your tenants and their rental history. This includes keeping a record of rent payments, maintenance requests, and any other issues that may arise. This will help you to make informed decisions about renewing leases and managing tenant turnover.

In conclusion, tenant management is an essential part of running a successful rental property business. By finding the right tenants, maintaining good relationships, enforcing rent collection policies, and keeping track of tenant history, you can maximize your ROI and ensure the long- term success of your rental property business.

Maximizing Return on Investment

Rent pricing strategies

Rent pricing strategies are an important aspect of rental property management. Determining the right rent price for your property can make or break your investment. The right rent price can attract quality tenants and maximize your ROI, while the wrong rent price can leave your property vacant or attract low-quality tenants. In this chapter, we will explore different rent pricing strategies that property investors can use to ensure they set the right rent price for their rental properties.

First, it is important to understand the market and the competition. Conducting a market analysis can help you determine the average rent price in your area and the rental rates of similar properties. This information can guide you in setting a competitive rent price that is not too high or too low.

Second, you can use the 1% rule. This rule suggests that you should charge 1% of the total value of your property as monthly rent. For example, if your property is worth $500,000, you should charge $5,000 in rent. This rule is useful for determining a baseline rent price, but it may not always be applicable depending on the market and competition.

Third, you can use the income approach. This approach involves calculating the rental income that your property is expected to generate based on its potential rental value, subtracting expenses such as property taxes, insurance, and maintenance, and arriving at a net operating income (NOI). You can then use the NOI to determine the rent price that will provide the desired return on investment.

Fourth, you can consider offering incentives to attract tenants and retain them. These incentives can include reduced rent for the first month, free utilities, or a discount for long-term leases.

Finally, it is important to regularly review and adjust rent prices to remain competitive and ensure that you are maximizing your ROI. By using these rent pricing strategies, property investors can set the right rent price for their rental properties and attract quality tenants while maximizing their ROI.

Property management software

Property management software has become an essential tool for property investors, landlords and property managers in recent years. The software enables them to keep track of their properties, tenants and finances in a way that is more efficient and less time-consuming than traditional methods.

There are many different types of property management software available, each with its own features and benefits. Some software is designed specifically for residential properties, while others are better suited for commercial or vacation properties.

One of the main benefits of property management software is that it allows investors and landlords to keep track of their finances more easily. They can keep track of rent payments, expenses, and other financial transactions all in one place, which can save time and reduce the likelihood of errors.

Another benefit of property management software is that it enables investors and landlords to communicate more effectively with their tenants. They can set up automated messages and reminders, send updates on maintenance work and repairs, and even share important documents like lease agreements and move-in checklists.

Many property management software systems also offer features like online rent payment, tenant screening, and maintenance tracking. These features can help investors and landlords save time and reduce the amount of paperwork they have to deal with.

While there are many benefits to using property management software, it is important to choose the right system for your needs. Some software can be expensive and may have more features than you need, while others may not offer the features you require.

Overall, property management software is an essential tool for property investors and landlords who want to maximize their ROI and streamline their operations. By choosing the right software and using it effectively, you can save time, reduce costs, and improve your bottom line.

Property upgrades
Tax deductions

When it comes to owning and managing rental properties, one important aspect that property investors need to understand is tax deductions. These are expenses that can be subtracted from your taxable rental income, which can help reduce your overall tax liability. In this subchapter, we will explore some of the most common tax deductions that property investors can take advantage of.

1. Mortgage interest - If you have a mortgage on your rental property, you can deduct the interest paid on that mortgage from your rental income. This is one of the biggest tax deductions available to property investors.

2. Property taxes - Another significant deduction is property taxes paid on your rental property. This deduction can help offset the cost of owning and managing your rental property.

3. Repairs and maintenance - Any expenses incurred for repairs and maintenance of your rental property can be deducted from your rental income. This can include things like fixing a leaky roof, painting the exterior of the property, or repairing a broken appliance.

4. Depreciation - Rental properties can be depreciated over time, which means you can deduct a portion of the property's value each year. This deduction can help offset the cost of owning and maintaining your rental property.

5. Home office expenses - If you use a portion of your home as an office for managing your rental properties, you can deduct expenses related to that home office. This can include things like internet and phone bills, office supplies, and even a portion of your rent or mortgage.

6. Travel expenses - If you need to travel to your rental property for maintenance or management purposes, you can deduct those travel expenses. This can include things like gas, lodging, and meals.

By taking advantage of these tax deductions, property investors can reduce their taxable rental income and save money on their taxes. However, it's important to keep accurate records and consult with a tax professional to ensure you are taking advantage of all possible deductions while staying in compliance with tax laws and regulations.

Property marketing

Property marketing is an essential skill for any property investor looking to maximize their ROI. Marketing your rental property effectively will attract quality tenants, reduce vacancy rates, and ultimately increase your bottom line. In this subchapter, we will discuss the key strategies for effective property marketing.

The first step in property marketing is identifying your target audience. Who are you trying to appeal to? Families, young professionals, retirees, or students? Once you have identified your target audience, you can tailor your marketing strategy to reach them effectively.

The most effective marketing strategy is to list your property on multiple platforms. This includes online rental websites, social media, and local classifieds. Online rental websites like Zillow, Trulia, and Apartments.com are excellent platforms to reach a large audience. These websites allow you to list your property, add photos, and describe the features and amenities of your property.

Social media is also a powerful tool for property marketing. Platforms like Facebook, Twitter, and Instagram allow you to post photos, videos, and descriptions of your property. You can also target your audience by location, age, and interests.

Another effective strategy is to use professional photos and videos. High-quality photos and videos will showcase your property in the best possible light and attract more potential tenants. A professional photographer can help you capture the best features of your property and create a compelling visual story.

Finally, it's essential to keep your property well-maintained and clean. A clean and well- maintained property will attract quality tenants and help you retain them for longer periods. Keep the property up-to-date with regular maintenance and upgrades, and ensure that it's always clean and presentable.

In conclusion, effective property marketing is essential for any property investor looking to maximize their ROI. By identifying your target audience, listing your property on multiple platforms, using professional photos and videos, and keeping your property well-maintained, you can attract quality tenants and increase your bottom line.

Commercial Rental Property

Overview of Commercial Property

Commercial property is a broad term that encompasses a wide range of properties, including offices, retail spaces, warehouses, and industrial spaces. This type of property is primarily used for business purposes and can be owned by individuals or corporations.

Investing in commercial property can be a lucrative venture for property investors looking to diversify their portfolio and increase their cash flow. However, commercial property investment comes with its own set of unique challenges and considerations that are different from residential property investment.

One of the key differences between commercial and residential property is the leasing process. Commercial leases are typically longer than residential leases, with terms that can range from three to ten years or more. This means that commercial property investors must be prepared to commit to long-term tenants and have a solid understanding of market trends to ensure that they are getting the best possible rent rates.

Another important consideration when investing in commercial property is the location. The location of a commercial property is critical to its success, as it can impact foot traffic, accessibility, and overall business operations. Commercial property investors must carefully evaluate the market demand and competition in the area to ensure that they are investing in a property that is in demand and has the potential for growth.

In addition to location, commercial property investors must also consider the type of property they are investing in. Different types of commercial properties have different risks and rewards, and investors must carefully weigh the pros and cons of each type before making a decision. For example, investing in a retail space may offer higher rent rates, but comes with greater competition and higher vacancy rates. On the other hand, investing in an industrial space may offer lower rent rates, but is generally less volatile and has lower vacancy rates.

Overall, investing in commercial property can be a rewarding and profitable venture for property investors. However, it requires a solid understanding of the market, careful consideration of location and property type, and a long-term commitment to tenants. By carefully evaluating these factors and developing a sound investment strategy, property investors can maximize their ROI and achieve long-term success in the commercial property market.

Types of commercial property

As a property investor, it is essential to understand the different types of commercial property available in the market. Commercial properties are buildings or spaces that generate income through rent or lease agreements. The types of commercial property include:

1. Office Buildings: These are buildings designed to house offices for businesses, organizations, and government agencies. Office buildings come in different sizes and classes, ranging from Class A (high-end buildings) to Class C (older buildings in less

desirable locations).

2. Retail Spaces: These are buildings or spaces designed for businesses to sell goods and services to the public. Retail spaces include shopping malls, strip malls, and standalone stores.

3. Industrial Properties: These are buildings used for manufacturing, storage, and distribution of goods. Industrial properties include warehouses, factories, and distribution centers.

4. Multi-Family Properties: These are buildings designed to house multiple families in individual apartments or units. Multi-family properties include apartment buildings, townhouses, and condominiums.

5. Hospitality Properties: These are properties designed for short-term stays such as hotels, motels, and resorts.

6. Healthcare Properties: These are properties designed for medical services and include hospitals, medical clinics, and nursing homes.

7. Mixed-Use Properties: These are properties that combine two or more types of commercial properties. For example, a mixed-use property may have retail spaces on the ground floor with apartments on the upper floors.

Each type of commercial property has its unique advantages and disadvantages. As a property investor, you must carefully analyze the market demand, location, and potential returns before investing in any commercial property.

In conclusion, understanding the different types of commercial properties can help you make informed investment decisions. As you venture into commercial property investing, consider taking a commercial property course to gain more knowledge and expertise in this lucrative sector.

Commercial property financing

Commercial property financing is a crucial aspect of real estate investing, especially for those looking to expand their portfolio into larger-scale properties. Commercial properties include office buildings, retail spaces, industrial warehouses, and multifamily apartment complexes. These types of properties require significant capital investment, making financing a critical component of the investment process.

There are several financing options available for commercial properties, including traditional bank loans, private lenders, and government-backed programs. Each option has its own set of pros and cons, and it's essential to understand the different financing options to make an informed decision.

Traditional bank loans are the most common financing method for commercial properties. These loans typically have longer repayment terms than residential loans, ranging from 10 to 30 years. The interest rates are also higher, and the borrower must have a strong credit score and financial history to qualify. However, bank loans offer the most competitive rates, making them an attractive option for investors who can meet the qualification requirements.

Private lenders are another option for commercial property financing. These lenders are typically individuals or companies that specialize in lending to real estate investors. Private lenders can offer more flexible terms than traditional banks, such as shorter repayment terms and higher loan-to-value ratios. However, the interest rates are usually higher than bank loans, and the borrower may need to provide collateral or a personal guarantee to secure the loan.

Government-backed programs, such as Small Business Administration (SBA) loans, are also available for commercial property financing. These programs are designed to help small businesses, including real estate investors, obtain financing. SBA loans have longer repayment terms than traditional bank loans and lower down payment requirements. However, the application process can be more complex and time-consuming than other financing options.

In conclusion, commercial property financing is a critical component of real estate investing. Understanding the different financing options available can help investors make informed decisions and maximize their return on investment. Whether you choose a traditional bank loan, private lender, or government-backed program, it's essential to do your research and work with a reputable lender to ensure a successful investment.

Commercial property management

Commercial property management is a vital aspect of real estate investing. Unlike residential properties, commercial properties require a different approach to management, and it is essential to have the right team in place to ensure that your investment is profitable. This section will cover everything you need to know about commercial property management, including what it entails, why it is important, and how to find the right property management team for your commercial investment.

Commercial property management involves managing and overseeing the day-to-day operations of a commercial property, which may include office buildings, retail centers, industrial buildings, and warehouses. This includes everything from tenant relations and rent collection to maintenance and repairs. The primary goal of commercial property management is to ensure that the property is profitable and well-maintained, and that tenants are satisfied with their rental experience.

One of the most significant benefits of commercial property management is that it can help maximize your ROI. By hiring a professional property management team, you can ensure that your property is always in top condition and that tenants are happy and willing to renew their leases. This can lead to increased rental income and a higher return on your investment.

When it comes to finding the right commercial property management team, there are a few things to keep in mind. First, look for a company with experience managing commercial properties similar to yours. They should have a proven track record of success and be able to provide references from satisfied clients.

Second, make sure that the property management team you choose has a comprehensive understanding of the local market and the specific needs of commercial tenants. They should be able to provide you with expert advice on how to market your property, attract high-quality tenants, and maximize your rental income.

Finally, look for a property management team that is responsive and easy to work with. They should be available to answer your questions and address any concerns you may have, and they should be willing to work with you to develop a customized management plan that meets your specific needs and goals.

In summary, commercial property management is a critical aspect of real estate investing. By hiring a professional property management team, you can ensure that your investment is profitable, well-maintained, and attractive to high-quality tenants. Keep these tips in mind when selecting a property management team for your commercial investment, and you'll be well on your way to success in the world of real estate investing.

Commercial property marketing

Commercial property marketing is an essential aspect of real estate investing. It involves promoting and advertising commercial properties to potential tenants or buyers. Effective marketing strategies can help property investors attract the right tenants, maximize their ROI, and boost their profits.

One of the most important aspects of commercial property marketing is understanding your target audience. Different types of commercial properties attract different types of tenants. For example, retail spaces may attract small business owners, while office spaces may appeal to larger corporations. Knowing your target audience can help you tailor your marketing efforts to their needs and preferences.

Another key aspect of commercial property marketing is creating a strong online presence. In today's digital age, most people start their property search online. As a property investor, it's important to have a well-designed website that showcases your properties and provides all the necessary information for potential tenants or buyers. Additionally, you should consider listing your properties on popular real estate platforms such as Zillow, LoopNet, and CoStar.

Networking is also crucial in commercial property marketing. Building relationships with other real estate professionals, such as brokers, property managers, and contractors, can help you expand your reach and find potential tenants or buyers. Attending industry events and joining local real estate associations can also help you stay up-to-date on industry trends and connect with potential clients.

Finally, offering incentives and promotions can help attract tenants and close deals quickly. Offering rent discounts or free rent periods can be an effective way to entice potential tenants. Additionally, offering move-in bonuses or covering the cost of renovations can make your property more appealing to buyers.

In conclusion, commercial property marketing is a critical component of real estate investing. By understanding your target audience, building a strong online presence, networking with other industry professionals, and offering incentives, you can attract the right tenants or buyers and maximize your ROI.

Residential Rental Property

Overview of Residential Property

Residential property refers to any property that is used for living purposes, such as single-family homes, apartments, townhouses, and condominiums. Residential property is one of the most popular and lucrative types of real estate investments. This is because people always need a place to live, and rental properties provide a stable source of income for property investors.

Investing in residential properties can be a profitable venture, but it requires careful planning and research. Before investing in any residential property, it is important to consider factors such as location, property condition, and the local rental market.

Location is one of the most important factors to consider when investing in residential property. A property located in a desirable neighborhood with good schools, transportation, and amenities is likely to attract high-quality tenants and generate higher rental income. It is also important to consider the local rental market and the level of demand for rental properties in the area.

The condition of the property is another important factor to consider. It is important to ensure that the property is in good condition and does not require extensive repairs or renovations. This will help to minimize maintenance costs and ensure that the property remains attractive to tenants.

Investing in residential property also requires careful management and maintenance. Property management is the process of overseeing the day-to-day operations of a rental property, including tenant screening, rent collection, and maintenance. Effective property management can help to maximize rental income and ensure that the property remains in good condition.

In conclusion, residential property is a popular and lucrative type of real estate investment. It is important to carefully consider factors such as location, property condition, and property management before investing in any residential property. With careful planning and research, residential property can provide a stable source of income for property investors.

Types of residential property

When it comes to residential property investments, there are several types of properties that investors can consider. Understanding the different types can help investors make informed decisions and maximize their ROI. Below are some of the most common types of residential properties:

1. Single-family homes: These are standalone homes designed to house one family. They can be rented out to a single tenant or a family. Single-family homes are often preferred by tenants who value privacy and space.

2. Multi-family homes: These are properties that house multiple families in separate units. They can range from duplexes to large

apartment complexes. Multi-family homes are typically more expensive to purchase but can provide a higher rental income.

3. Condominiums: These are individual units within a larger building or complex. Condos are typically owned by individuals who pay a monthly fee for maintenance and upkeep of the building. Condos can be rented out to tenants, but investors should be aware of any rules and regulations set by the condo association.

4. Townhouses: These are similar to single-family homes but are usually attached to other units. Townhouses are often more affordable than single-family homes and can be a good option for investors looking to purchase multiple units.

5. Vacation rentals: These are properties that are rented out to vacationers on a short-term basis. They can be located in popular tourist destinations or in areas with seasonal attractions. Vacation rentals can provide a high rental income but require careful management and upkeep.

6. Luxury properties: These are high-end properties that typically offer luxurious amenities and features. Luxury properties can provide a high rental income but require a significant investment.

Investors should consider their budget, location, and target market when choosing a residential property type. Each type of property has its own advantages and disadvantages, and investors should carefully weigh these factors before making a purchase. By understanding the different types of residential properties, investors can make informed decisions and maximize their ROI.

Residential property financing

Residential property financing is a crucial aspect of real estate investing. It is the process of securing funds to purchase or renovate a residential property. As a property investor, it is important to have a clear understanding of the different financing options available to you.

The most common form of residential property financing is a mortgage loan. This is a loan that is secured by the property being purchased. The terms of the loan vary depending on the lender, but typically include a down payment requirement, interest rate, and repayment schedule.

Another option for financing a residential property is a home equity loan or line of credit. This type of loan allows you to borrow against the equity you have built up in your current home.

This can be a good option for investors who have a significant amount of equity in their primary residence.

Another financing option for residential properties is a hard money loan. This type of loan is typically used for fix-and-flip projects where the property will be renovated and sold quickly. Hard money loans have higher interest rates and shorter repayment terms, but can be a good option for investors who need funds quickly.

In addition to traditional financing options, there are also alternative financing options available to investors. Crowdfunding, for example, allows investors to pool their money together to fund a project. This can be a good option for investors who do not have the capital to fund a project on their own.

When considering residential property financing options, it is important to consider the risks and benefits of each option. It is also important to work with a reputable lender who understands the unique needs of real estate investors.

In conclusion, residential property financing is a critical aspect of real estate investing. As a property investor, it is important to understand the different financing options available and to work with a reputable lender to secure the funds needed to purchase or renovate a property. By doing so, investors can maximize their ROI and build a successful real estate portfolio.

Residential property management

Residential property management is one of the most crucial components of real estate investing. It is an essential aspect of owning rental properties, as managing your properties well can ultimately determine your success as an investor. Proper management can lead to happy tenants, increased property value, and maximum ROI.

To be a successful residential property manager, you must have excellent communication skills, be detail-oriented, and have a thorough understanding of the local rental market. You must also be able to handle maintenance issues, rent collection, and tenant disputes effectively.

One of the most important aspects of residential property management is finding the right tenants. The screening process must be thorough, including a background check, credit check, and rental history verification. This can help ensure that your tenants are reliable and responsible, reducing the risk of late payments and property damage.

Rent collection is another crucial part of property management. You must establish a system that is easy for tenants to use and ensures timely payments. Late or missed payments can significantly impact your ROI, so it is important to be proactive in collecting rent and addressing any issues promptly.

Maintenance is another significant aspect of residential property management. Regular maintenance can prevent minor issues from turning into costly repairs. You must also respond promptly to tenant requests for repairs or maintenance issues. This can help build trust with your tenants, leading to long-term relationships and increased ROI.

Tenant disputes and evictions can be a challenging part of property management. You must have a thorough understanding of local landlord-tenant laws to ensure that you handle disputes and evictions legally and professionally. It is essential to have a written lease agreement that outlines the expectations and responsibilities of both parties. This can help prevent disputes and provide a clear framework for resolving any issues that may arise.

In conclusion, residential property management is an essential aspect of real estate investing. Proper management can lead to happy tenants, reduced vacancy rates, and maximum ROI. To be a successful property manager, you must possess excellent communication skills, be detail-oriented, and have a thorough understanding of the local rental market. By focusing on finding the right tenants, collecting rent on time, maintaining your property, and handling disputes professionally, you can ensure that your rental property is a profitable investment.

Residential property marketing

Marketing your residential property is essential to attract potential tenants, maximize your return on investment, and keep your property occupied. Effective marketing strategies can ensure that your property stands out in a crowded rental market, increasing its visibility and appeal.

One of the most important aspects of residential property marketing is understanding your target audience. Who are you trying to attract? Are you targeting students, young professionals, families, or retirees? Each group has unique needs and preferences that should be considered when developing your marketing plan. For example, students may prioritize proximity to campus and affordability, while families may prioritize access to good schools and safe neighborhoods.

Once you have identified your target audience, you can begin to tailor your marketing efforts accordingly. One effective strategy is to create a compelling online listing that showcases the unique features and benefits of your property. This can include high-quality photos, detailed descriptions of the amenities and location, and virtual tours if possible.

Social media can also be a powerful tool for residential property marketing. By creating a social media presence for your property and engaging with potential tenants, you can build a strong brand identity and foster a sense of community among your tenants.

Another effective marketing strategy is to partner with local businesses or organizations that cater to your target audience. For example, if you are targeting young professionals, you could partner with local gyms or cafes to offer discounted memberships or promotions to your tenants.

Ultimately, the key to successful residential property marketing is to be creative, strategic, and proactive. By understanding your target audience, identifying the most effective marketing channels, and continually refining your approach, you can attract high-quality tenants and maximize your return on investment.

Real Estate Development

Overview of Real Estate Development

Real estate development is the process of creating new buildings, structures, or communities from raw land or existing properties. It involves a wide range of activities including market analysis, design, financing, construction, and marketing. Real estate developers are responsible for coordinating all of these activities to ensure that the project is completed on time, within budget, and to the desired specifications.

Real estate development is a complex and dynamic field that requires a diverse set of skills and knowledge. Successful developers must have a deep understanding of the local real estate market, zoning laws and regulations, construction methods and materials, financing options, and marketing strategies. They must also be able to manage multiple stakeholders, including investors, contractors, architects, government officials, and community members.

Real estate development projects can range in size from small residential renovations to large- scale commercial developments. Some common types of development projects include:

Residential development: This involves building new homes, apartments, or condominiums. Residential developers must consider factors such as location, design, amenities, and pricing to attract potential buyers or renters.

Commercial development: This includes projects such as office buildings, retail centers, and industrial parks. Commercial developers must identify market demand, design functional and attractive spaces, and secure tenants or buyers.

Mixed-use development: This involves combining multiple types of properties, such as residential, commercial, and retail, into a single development. Mixed-use projects can create vibrant communities that offer a variety of amenities and services.

Real estate development can be a lucrative investment opportunity for property investors, but it also comes with significant risks. Developers must carefully manage their finances and timelines to ensure that they can complete the project and generate a profit. They must also be prepared to navigate potential setbacks such as zoning issues, construction delays, and changes in market conditions.

If you are interested in learning more about real estate development, there are a variety of courses and resources available. A real estate development course can provide you with the knowledge and skills you need to succeed in this challenging field. Whether you are interested in residential or commercial development, there are many opportunities to explore and grow your real estate portfolio.

Steps in real estate development

Real estate development is a complex and multifaceted process that requires careful planning, extensive research, and a lot of hard work. Whether you are a seasoned property investor or just starting out in the field, understanding the steps involved in real estate development can help you navigate the process more effectively and maximize your ROI.

Step 1: Market Research

The first step in real estate development is conducting market research. This involves researching the local real estate market, identifying potential investment opportunities, and analyzing the demand for different types of properties. You should also consider factors such as zoning laws, building codes, and environmental regulations that may impact your development plans.

Step 2: Site Selection

Once you have identified potential investment opportunities, the next step is to select a suitable site for your development project. This involves considering factors such as location, accessibility, and the availability of essential utilities such as water, electricity, and sewerage.

Step 3: Design and Planning

The design and planning phase of real estate development involves creating a detailed blueprint for your project. This includes developing architectural plans, obtaining necessary permits and approvals, and ensuring that your project complies with all applicable laws and regulations.

Step 4: Financing

Financing is a critical aspect of real estate development, and it is essential to secure adequate funding for your project. This may involve obtaining loans, partnering with other investors, or raising capital through equity financing.

Step 5: Construction

The construction phase of real estate development involves building your project according to the plans and specifications outlined in the design and planning phase. This requires working with a team of contractors, builders, and other professionals to ensure that your project is completed on time, within budget, and to the highest quality standards.

Step 6: Marketing and Sales

Once your project is complete, the final step is to market and sell your properties. This involves developing a marketing strategy, working with real estate agents, and leveraging various online platforms and tools to reach potential buyers.

In conclusion, real estate development is a complex process that requires careful planning, extensive research, and a lot of hard work. By understanding the steps involved in real estate development, property investors can navigate the process more effectively and maximize their ROI. Whether you are interested in residential or commercial real estate development, taking a comprehensive real estate development course can provide you with the skills and knowledge you need to succeed in this exciting field.

Financing Real Estate Development

Real estate development is a complex and expensive process that requires significant financial investment. From acquiring land to obtaining necessary permits and approvals, to construction and marketing, the costs can quickly add up. As a property investor, you need to understand the various financing options available to you to ensure the success of your real estate development project.

Traditional Financing

Traditional financing options are available for real estate development, including bank loans, private loans, and lines of credit. These options require a substantial down payment, and you need to provide collateral in the form of your existing property or assets. The application process is lengthy, and lenders will scrutinize your credit score, financial history, and the feasibility of your project before approving your loan.

Crowdfunding

Crowdfunding has emerged as a popular alternative to traditional financing for real estate development. With crowdfunding, you can raise funds from a large pool of investors who contribute small amounts of money to your project. This option is ideal for investors who have a strong online presence and can leverage social media and other online platforms to attract investors.

Joint Venture Partnerships

Another financing option for real estate development is joint venture partnerships. This option involves partnering with another investor or developer who has the necessary resources and expertise to complete the project. In a joint venture partnership, you share the costs and profits of the project, and the partnership agreement outlines the responsibilities and expectations of each party.

Creative Financing

Creative financing options are available for real estate development, including seller financing, lease-to-own agreements, and equity financing. These options require negotiation skills and a thorough understanding of the legal and financial implications of each option.

Conclusion

Real estate development requires a significant financial investment, and as a property investor, you need to understand the various financing options available to you. Traditional financing, crowdfunding, joint venture partnerships, and creative financing are all viable options, and you need to weigh the pros and cons of each option before making a decision. By choosing the right financing option, you can ensure the success of your real estate development project and maximize your ROI.

Property management in real estate development

Property management is a crucial aspect of real estate development that requires careful planning and execution. It involves the supervision and maintenance of properties, ensuring that they are in good condition and generating maximum returns for the property owner. Property management involves various activities, including tenant screening, rent collection, maintenance, repairs, and marketing.

For property investors, effective property management is essential for maximizing return on investment (ROI). Whether you are investing in commercial or residential properties, managing your properties effectively can make a significant difference in your profitability. Effective property management involves understanding the needs of your tenants, maintaining your properties, and optimizing your rental income.

One of the key aspects of property management is tenant screening. Finding the right tenants requires a careful screening process that involves checking credit history, employment status, and rental history. Tenants who pay their rent on time and take care of your property can be invaluable assets to your real estate portfolio. On the other hand, tenants who damage your property, fail to pay rent, or cause other problems can be costly and time-consuming to deal with.

Rent collection is another essential aspect of property management. Collecting rent on time ensures that your cash flow remains healthy and that your property is generating the maximum revenue possible. Late rent payments can significantly affect your profitability, so it's crucial to have a system in place to ensure that rent is paid on time.

Maintenance and repairs are also critical components of property management. Keeping your properties in good condition ensures that they remain attractive to tenants and that you can command higher rents. Regular maintenance and repairs can also help prevent more significant problems from developing, which can be costly to fix.

Finally, marketing is an essential aspect of property management. Effective marketing can help attract the right tenants to your property, ensuring that your properties remain occupied and generating rental income. Marketing can involve various activities, including advertising, social media marketing, and networking.

In conclusion, effective property management is essential for maximizing ROI in real estate development. Whether you are investing in commercial or residential properties, managing your properties effectively requires careful planning and execution. By understanding the needs of your tenants, maintaining your properties, and optimizing your rental income, you can ensure that your real estate portfolio generates the maximum returns possible.

Marketing real estate development

Marketing real estate development is an essential aspect of property investment. It involves promoting and selling properties that are under construction or newly completed. The goal of marketing a real estate development is to attract potential buyers, investors, or tenants. In this subchapter, we will discuss the various marketing strategies that you can use to promote your real estate development.

One of the most effective ways to market your real estate development is through online marketing. You can use social media platforms such as Facebook, Twitter, and Instagram to promote your development. You can also create a website for your development where you can showcase the features and amenities of your property. You can use search engine optimization (SEO) techniques to ensure that your website ranks high in search engine results when potential buyers or investors search for properties in your area.

Another effective marketing strategy is to work with real estate agents and brokers. These professionals have extensive networks and can help you reach potential buyers or tenants. They can also provide valuable advice on pricing and marketing strategies.

You can also host events and open houses to showcase your property. This is a great way to attract potential buyers and investors and to give them a firsthand look at your development. You can also collaborate with local businesses and organizations to promote your property.

When marketing your real estate development, it is important to highlight the unique features and amenities of your property. This could include features such as high-end finishes, energy- efficient appliances, or smart home technology. You should also emphasize the location of your development and the surrounding neighborhood. This could include proximity to schools, shopping centers, and public transportation.

In conclusion, marketing real estate development is a crucial aspect of property investment. By using effective marketing strategies, you can attract potential buyers, investors, or tenants and maximize your ROI. Whether you are marketing a rental property, commercial property, or luxury property, the key is to highlight the unique features and amenities of your property and to reach out to potential buyers or tenants through a variety of channels.

Vacation and Short-Term Rentals

Overview of vacation and short-term rentals

Vacation and short-term rentals have become increasingly popular over the years. With more people traveling for leisure, business, and other purposes, the demand for vacation rentals has skyrocketed. Property investors are taking advantage of this trend by investing in vacation and short-term rental properties.

A vacation rental is a property that is rented out to travelers for a short period, usually for a week or less. These rentals can be anything from a single room in a house to an entire villa or apartment. They are usually fully furnished and equipped with all the necessary amenities, including kitchen appliances, Wi-Fi, and entertainment systems.

Short-term rentals, on the other hand, are similar to vacation rentals but are rented out for a shorter period. These rentals can be anything from a few days to a few weeks. They are also fully furnished and equipped with all the necessary amenities.

One of the advantages of investing in vacation and short-term rentals is the high rental income potential. These rentals can generate more income than long-term rentals, especially during peak travel seasons. They also offer property investors the flexibility to use the property for their own vacations or to rent it out as a long-term rental when there is low demand.

However, there are also some challenges associated with vacation and short-term rentals. One of the biggest challenges is managing the property. Property investors need to ensure that the property is always clean, well-maintained, and stocked with all the necessary supplies. They also need to manage the bookings, payments, and communication with the guests.

Another challenge is the legal and regulatory framework surrounding vacation and short-term rentals. Property investors need to comply with local laws and regulations, including zoning laws, safety regulations, and tax laws. Failure to comply with these laws can result in fines and legal action.

In conclusion, vacation and short-term rentals offer property investors a lucrative investment opportunity. However, it is important to understand the challenges associated with these rentals and to have a solid management plan in place to ensure their success.

Types of Vacation and Short-Term Rentals

Vacation rentals and short-term rentals are popular choices for travelers looking for alternative accommodations. These rental properties provide a unique experience, allowing guests to immerse themselves in the local community and culture. As a property investor, understanding the different types of vacation and short-term rentals can help you choose the right investment strategy.

1. Vacation Homes

Vacation homes are typically fully furnished properties that are rented out for short periods of time, usually a week or more. These homes can be located in popular tourist destinations, such as beach towns or ski resorts, and are often used as a second home by the property owner. Vacation homes can be rented out directly by the owner or through a property management company.

2. Short-Term Rentals

Short-term rentals are typically rented out for a few days to a few weeks and can include a variety of properties, such as apartments, condos, and homes. These rentals are often found in urban areas, such as city centers, and cater to travelers looking for a more authentic experience. Short-term rentals can also be rented out directly by the owner or through a property management company.

3. Corporate Rentals

Corporate rentals are short-term rentals that are typically used by business travelers. These rentals are often located near business districts and offer amenities such as high-speed internet and workspace. Corporate rentals can be rented out directly by the owner or through a property management company.

4. Bed and Breakfast

Bed and breakfasts are typically small, intimate properties that offer accommodations and breakfast to guests. These rentals can be found in both urban and rural areas and are often run by the property owner. Bed and breakfasts can also be rented out through a property management company.

5. Timeshares

Timeshares are a type of vacation ownership that allows guests to own a share of a property for a specific period of time, usually a week or more. Timeshares can be found in popular tourist destinations and can be rented out when the owner is not using them.

Understanding the different types of vacation and short-term rentals can help you choose the right investment strategy. Whether you are looking to invest in a vacation home or short-term rental, it is important to consider the location, amenities, and target market before making a decision. With the right strategy, vacation and short-term rentals can provide a profitable investment opportunity.

Financing vacation and short-term rentals

Financing vacation and short-term rentals can be a bit more challenging than traditional rental properties, as they require a different approach to financing. In this subchapter, we'll explore the various financing options available to property investors looking to invest in vacation and short-term rentals.

One of the most popular financing options for vacation and short-term rentals is a conventional mortgage. These mortgages are typically offered by banks and lending institutions and require a down payment of 20% or more. While these mortgages are widely available, they can be more difficult to obtain for non-traditional rental properties. This is because lenders typically view vacation rentals as riskier investments than traditional rentals.

Another financing option for vacation and short-term rentals is a commercial loan. These loans are typically offered by banks and lending institutions and are specifically designed for non- traditional rental properties. Commercial loans typically offer higher loan amounts than conventional mortgages, but they also come with higher interest rates and stricter lending requirements.

If you're looking to finance a vacation or short-term rental property, you may also want to consider a home equity loan or line of credit. These loans allow you to borrow against your existing home equity to finance your rental property. While they can be a good option for financing a vacation rental, they can also be risky, as you're putting your home equity on the line.

Finally, if you're looking to finance a vacation or short-term rental property, you may want to consider crowdfunding. Crowdfunding platforms allow you to raise money from a large group of investors to fund your rental property. While this can be a good option for those who don't have the capital to invest on their own, it can be a risky option, as you're relying on the success of your rental property to pay back your investors.

In conclusion, financing vacation and short-term rentals can be a bit more challenging than traditional rental properties. However, by exploring the various financing options available to you, you can find the right financing option to help you invest in your dream rental property.

Vacation and short-term rental management

Vacation and short-term rental management can be a lucrative way to invest in real estate. With the rise of platforms like Airbnb and VRBO, more and more travelers are opting for vacation rentals over traditional hotels. If you're considering investing in a vacation or short-term rental property, it's important to understand the unique challenges and opportunities that come with this type of investment.

One of the biggest benefits of vacation rentals is the potential for higher rental income. Because these properties are rented out for shorter periods of time, they can often command higher nightly rates than long-term rental properties. Additionally, vacation rentals can be rented out for more weeks out of the year, which means more potential rental income.

However, managing a vacation rental requires a different approach than managing a long-term rental property. With short-term rentals, turnover is much higher, and you'll need to be prepared to clean and prepare the property for each new guest. You'll also need to be available to answer questions and address any issues that arise during your guests' stay.

To successfully manage a vacation or short-term rental property, it's important to have a solid marketing and booking strategy in place. You'll need to create an attractive listing that highlights the unique features of your property and appeals to potential guests. You'll also need to be prepared to handle booking inquiries and manage reservations.

Another important aspect of vacation rental management is ensuring that your property is compliant with local laws and regulations. Depending on where your property is located, there may be restrictions on short-term rentals or requirements for things like occupancy taxes or licensing.

Overall, vacation and short-term rental management can be a rewarding investment opportunity for property investors. By understanding the unique challenges and opportunities of this type of investment, you can maximize your rental income and provide a great experience for your guests.

Marketing Vacation and Short-Term Rentals

Marketing is an essential aspect of vacation and short-term rentals. The success of your rental property depends on your ability to attract and retain guests. In this subchapter, we will discuss the different marketing strategies that you can use to promote your vacation and short-term rentals.

1. Online Listing Platforms

Online listing platforms, such as Airbnb, Vrbo, and Booking.com, are some of the most popular and effective ways to market vacation and short-term rentals. These platforms have a wide reach, and they allow you to showcase your property to a global audience. They also provide various tools and features to help you manage your listing, including pricing, availability, and communication with guests.

When creating your listing, make sure to highlight the unique features of your property and provide detailed information about the amenities, location, and nearby attractions. Use high- quality photos to showcase your property and make it stand out from the competition.

2. Social Media

Social media is another effective marketing tool for vacation and short-term rentals. Platforms like Facebook and Instagram allow you to reach a targeted audience and connect with potential guests. You can use social media to showcase your property, share guest reviews and feedback, and promote special offers and discounts.

Make sure to use relevant hashtags to increase your reach and engage with your followers by responding to comments and messages promptly. You can also collaborate with local businesses and influencers to expand your reach and attract new guests.

3. Email Marketing

Email marketing is a powerful way to stay in touch with past guests and promote your property to potential guests. You can use email marketing to send newsletters, special offers, and updates about your property and the surrounding area.

Make sure to collect email addresses from your guests and use a professional email marketing tool to create targeted and personalized campaigns. You can also use email marketing to solicit guest feedback and reviews, which can help improve your property's reputation and attract new guests.

In conclusion, marketing is a crucial aspect of vacation and short-term rentals. By using online listing platforms, social media, and email marketing, you can attract and retain guests and maximize the ROI of your rental property.

Real Estate Flipping

Overview of Real Estate Flipping

Real estate flipping is a popular investment strategy in the world of real estate, where investors purchase a property with the intention of renovating it and then selling it at a higher price. This process involves purchasing a property that is in a state of disrepair, fixing it up, and selling it for a profit. Flipping can be done with both residential and commercial properties, and it can be a great way for investors to make a quick return on their investment.

Flipping a property involves several steps, including finding the right property, financing the purchase, renovating the property, and then selling it. The first step is finding the right property. Investors need to find properties that are undervalued, have potential for appreciation, and are in a desirable location. Once the property is identified, the investor must obtain financing for the purchase. This can be done through traditional lenders, private lenders, or through their own personal funds.

The next step is renovating the property. This involves making repairs, upgrading the property with modern amenities, and making it more appealing to potential buyers. The renovation process can vary depending on the property and the investor's goals. Some investors may choose to make small cosmetic changes, while others may choose to completely gut the property and rebuild it from scratch.

Once the renovation is complete, the property is put on the market for sale. The investor must price the property correctly in order to attract potential buyers. It is important to understand the local real estate market and to price the property to sell quickly. Once the property is sold, the investor makes a profit on the sale.

Flipping can be a lucrative investment strategy, but it does come with risks. Investors must have a solid understanding of the real estate market, be able to accurately estimate renovation costs, and be willing to take on the financial risk of the investment. However, with careful planning and execution, real estate flipping can be a great way for investors to make a quick return on their investment.

Steps in real estate flipping

Real estate flipping is the process of buying a property, making improvements to it, and then selling it for a profit. While it may seem like a simple process, there are many steps involved in successfully flipping a property. If you're considering getting into the world of real estate flipping, here are the steps you should follow:

Step 1: Define your goals and budget

Before you start looking for properties to flip, you need to define your goals and budget. How much money do you have to invest? What kind of profit do you want to make? What kind of property are you looking for? These are all important questions to answer before you start searching for properties.

Step 2: Find a property to flip

Once you have defined your goals and budget, it's time to start looking for a property to flip. You can find properties through real estate agents, online listings, or by driving around and looking for properties with "For Sale" signs.

Step 3: Evaluate the property

Once you have found a property that you're interested in flipping, you need to evaluate it to determine if it's a good investment. Look at the condition of the property, the neighborhood, and the potential for resale value.

Step 4: Secure financing

Once you have evaluated the property and determined that it's a good investment, you need to secure financing. You can do this through a traditional lender, such as a bank, or through private financing.

Step 5: Make improvements

Once you have secured financing, it's time to make improvements to the property. This can include anything from cosmetic upgrades to major renovations.

Step 6: Market the property

Once the improvements have been made, it's time to market the property to potential buyers. This can be done through real estate agents, online listings, or by holding an open house.

Step 7: Sell the property

Once you have found a buyer, it's time to sell the property. Make sure you have all the necessary paperwork in order and that the closing process goes smoothly.

Flipping a property can be a lucrative investment, but it's important to follow these steps to ensure that you're making a smart investment and maximizing your profit potential.

Financing real estate flipping

Real estate flipping can be a lucrative business, but it requires a significant amount of capital to get started. Financing is a critical component of real estate flipping that can make or break a deal. In this subchapter, we will explore different financing options available to real estate flippers.

1. Traditional bank loans

Traditional bank loans are the most common financing option for real estate flippers. Typically, banks require a down payment of 20% to 30% of the property's value and a good credit score. The interest rates on bank loans are generally low, making them an attractive option for flippers. However, the loan process can be lengthy, and approval is not guaranteed.

2. Hard money loans

Hard money loans are short-term loans that are secured by the property being flipped. The interest rates on hard money loans are higher than traditional bank loans, but the approval process is much faster. Hard money lenders do not require a good credit score, but they do require a significant down payment, usually 30% to 50% of the property's value. Hard money loans are a good option for flippers who need quick access to capital.

3. Private money loans

Private money loans are loans from individuals rather than institutions. Private money lenders are often real estate investors themselves and understand the business of flipping. Private money loans generally have higher interest rates than traditional bank loans, but they are more flexible in terms of loan terms and approval criteria.

4. Crowdfunding

Crowdfunding is a relatively new financing option for real estate flippers. Crowdfunding platforms allow investors to pool their money together to fund a real estate project.

Crowdfunding is an attractive option for flippers who do not have access to traditional financing or who do not want to take on the risk of a loan. However, crowdfunding platforms charge fees, and the approval process can be competitive.

In conclusion, financing is a crucial component of real estate flipping. Flippers must consider their options carefully to find the financing that best fits their needs. Traditional bank loans, hard money loans, private money loans, and crowdfunding are all viable options for flippers. By selecting the right financing option, flippers can maximize their return on investment and build a successful real estate flipping business.

Property management in real estate flipping
Marketing real estate flipping

Marketing is a critical aspect of real estate flipping. As a property investor, you need to know how to effectively market your investment property to attract potential buyers and maximize your ROI. In this chapter, we will discuss some essential marketing strategies and techniques that you can implement to successfully flip your property.

1. Know your target market

The first step to effectively market your flipping property is to understand your target market. Who are the potential buyers? What are their needs, preferences, and budget? Once you have identified your target market, you can tailor your marketing strategies to meet their specific needs and preferences.

2. Create an attractive listing

Your property listing is the first impression that potential buyers will have of your flipping property. It is therefore critical to create a professional and attractive listing that showcases your property's unique features, amenities, and benefits. Include high-quality photos and videos, a detailed description of the property, and accurate pricing information.

3. Use social media

Social media is a powerful marketing tool that can help you reach a broader audience and generate more leads. Use platforms like Facebook, Instagram, Twitter, and LinkedIn to promote your flipping property and engage with potential buyers. You can also use social media ads to target specific audiences and increase your visibility.

4. Partner with real estate agents

Real estate agents have vast networks and can help you market your flipping property to potential buyers. Partner with reputable agents in your area and provide them with all the necessary information about your property. They can then showcase your property to their clients and help you find potential buyers quickly.

5. Offer incentives

Offering incentives can motivate potential buyers to take action and purchase your flipping property. You can offer incentives like discounts, free upgrades, or a home warranty to entice potential buyers and differentiate your property from others in the market.

In conclusion, marketing is a critical aspect of real estate flipping. By understanding your target market, creating an attractive listing, using social media, partnering with real estate agents, and offering incentives, you can successfully market your flipping property and maximize your ROI.

Luxury Property Rental

Overview of Luxury Property Rental

Luxury property rental is a niche market within the real estate industry that caters to high-end clients who are seeking short-term or long-term accommodation in exclusive and upscale locations. Luxury properties are typically characterized by their unique architecture, high-end finishes, and premium amenities such as swimming pools, spas, and fitness centers.

The demand for luxury property rental has been on the rise in recent years, with more and more people looking for a luxurious and hassle-free alternative to traditional hotel stays. Luxury property rental is particularly popular among affluent travelers, business executives, and high- net-worth individuals who value privacy, exclusivity, and personalized service.

If you are a property investor looking to enter the luxury property rental market, there are several factors that you need to consider.

Firstly, you need to identify the right location. Luxury properties are typically located in prime areas such as beachfronts, mountainsides, or city centers. These locations offer stunning views, convenient access to local attractions, and a sense of exclusivity that appeals to high-end clients.

Secondly, you need to select the right property. Luxury properties come in a variety of shapes and sizes, ranging from lavish villas to penthouses, to sprawling estates. The key is to choose a property that offers the right balance of luxury, functionality, and practicality. You also need to consider the property's maintenance and upkeep costs, as luxury properties require regular maintenance and upkeep to maintain their high standards.

Thirdly, you need to provide exceptional service. Luxury property rental is all about providing a personalized and seamless experience for your clients. This includes offering concierge services, personal chefs, private transportation, and other amenities that cater to your clients' specific needs and preferences.

Lastly, you need to market your property effectively. Luxury property rental is a competitive market, and you need to stand out from the crowd to attract high-end clients. This includes creating a professional website, using high-quality photos and videos, and leveraging social media and other online channels to reach your target audience.

In conclusion, luxury property rental is a lucrative and rewarding niche within the real estate industry that requires careful planning, investment, and attention to detail. By following the tips outlined above and staying up-to-date with the latest trends and developments in the market, you can build a successful and profitable luxury property rental business that caters to the needs of high-end clients.

Types of Luxury Property Rental

Luxury property rentals are a great way to enjoy a high-end lifestyle without having to commit to buying a property. They offer a level of comfort, convenience, and exclusivity that is hard to match in other types of rentals. If you are a property investor looking to expand your portfolio and cater to high-end clients, here are some types of luxury property rentals that you should consider.

1. Vacation Rentals

Vacation rentals are a popular choice for luxury travelers who want to stay in a home-like environment, rather than a hotel. These properties are often located in prime vacation destinations, such as beachfronts, ski resorts, or exotic locations. They can range from cozy villas to expansive mansions, with amenities like private pools, hot tubs, game rooms, and outdoor spaces.

2. Short-term Rentals

Short-term rentals are similar to vacation rentals, but they cater to a broader range of clients, including business travelers, event attendees, and people relocating to a new city. They can be furnished apartments, penthouses, or townhouses, with services like housekeeping, concierge, and transportation. Short-term rentals can be a lucrative investment, especially in high-demand cities or during peak seasons.

3. Corporate Rentals

Corporate rentals are a specialized type of short-term rental that caters to business travelers who need a temporary home base for a project, conference, or training. They are usually furnished apartments or condominiums, with amenities like high-speed internet, office space, and conference rooms. Corporate rentals can provide a steady income stream, as they are often booked by companies for extended periods of time.

4. Event Rentals

Event rentals are luxury properties that are rented out for special occasions, such as weddings, parties, or retreats. They can be castles, mansions, or estates, with elegant décor, spacious grounds, and catering services. Event rentals can be a niche investment, as they require specialized marketing and management, but they can yield high profits during peak seasons.

5. High-end Residential Rentals

High-end residential rentals are luxury apartments or homes that cater to affluent tenants who want a lavish lifestyle without the commitment of buying a property. They can be located in prime neighborhoods, with amenities like fitness centers, theaters, and private clubs. High-end residential rentals require a significant investment, but they can provide long-term stability and appreciation, as well as tax benefits.

In conclusion, luxury property rentals offer a diverse range of investment opportunities, from vacation homes to high-end apartments. As a property investor, it is essential to research the market, identify your target clients, and tailor your properties to their specific needs and preferences. With the right strategy and management, luxury property rentals can provide a steady income stream, appreciation, and prestige.

Financing Luxury Property Rental

Investing in luxury property rental can be a lucrative opportunity for property investors. However, financing such a venture may require more effort and resources compared to traditional real estate investments. In this subchapter, we will explore various financing options available to investors interested in luxury property rental.

One of the most common ways to finance luxury property rental is through a mortgage. However, since luxury properties come with a higher price tag, lenders may have stricter requirements for borrowers. Investors may need to have a higher credit score, a larger down payment, and a lower debt-to-income ratio to qualify for a mortgage. Additionally, lenders may require a higher interest rate for luxury property rental loans.

Another option for financing luxury property rental is through a real estate investment trust (REIT). A REIT is a company that owns and manages a portfolio of income-generating real estate properties. Investors can buy shares in a REIT and earn dividends from the rental income generated by the properties owned by the trust. REITs offer investors an opportunity to invest in luxury properties without the hassle of managing the property themselves.

Private equity firms and crowdfunding platforms also offer financing options for luxury property rental. Private equity firms invest in real estate projects and offer financing to property investors. Crowdfunding platforms allow investors to pool their resources together and invest in luxury properties. Both options provide access to capital that may not be available through traditional financing methods.

Lastly, some investors may choose to finance luxury property rental through their own savings or by partnering with other investors. Self-financing allows investors to have more control over their investments and may offer more flexibility in terms of repayment. Partnering with other investors can also provide access to additional resources and expertise in managing luxury properties.

In conclusion, financing luxury property rental may require more effort and resources, but the potential returns can be significant. Investors should consider all available financing options and choose the one that best suits their financial situation and investment goals.

Luxury property management

Luxury property management is a specialized field that requires a unique set of skills and expertise. It involves managing high-end properties that cater to the needs of the affluent and elite. The expectations of luxury property owners are high, and their demands are varied.

Therefore, luxury property management requires a deep understanding of the nuances of the luxury real estate market, as well as the ability to deliver exceptional service.

The goal of luxury property management is to ensure that the property is maintained to the highest standards, and the owner's investment is protected. This involves hiring a team of experts who can manage everything from maintenance and repairs to marketing and tenant relations.

The team should be knowledgeable, experienced, and well-trained in all aspects of luxury property management.

One of the most important aspects of luxury property management is tenant relations. Luxury property owners expect a high level of service, and their tenants are no exception. The property manager should be able to provide personalized service to each tenant, ensuring that their needs are met, and their expectations are exceeded. This may include arranging for private chefs, personal trainers, and other luxury services.

Another critical aspect of luxury property management is marketing. Luxury properties require a unique marketing approach that targets the right audience. The property manager should be able to develop a comprehensive marketing strategy that includes online advertising, social media, and other targeted marketing techniques.

Maintenance and repairs are also essential in luxury property management. Luxury properties require regular maintenance to ensure that they remain in top condition. The property manager should have a team of experienced professionals who can handle everything from routine maintenance to major repairs.

In conclusion, luxury property management is a specialized field that requires a deep understanding of the luxury real estate market. The property manager should be able to provide exceptional service, personalized attention, and a comprehensive marketing strategy. With the right team in place, luxury property owners can rest assured that their investment is in good hands.

Luxury property marketing

Luxury property marketing is a specialized field that requires a unique set of skills and strategies. It is one of the most competitive niches in the real estate industry and demands a high level of attention to detail, creativity, and a deep understanding of the target audience.

If you are a property investor looking to market a luxury property, you need to know what makes it stand out from other properties and how to showcase its unique features to attract the right buyers.

One of the first steps in luxury property marketing is identifying the ideal target market. This can be done by analyzing the property's location, amenities, and features to determine who would be the best fit for the property. For example, a luxury beachfront property would appeal to buyers who are looking for a vacation home or a place to retire, while a luxury downtown condo would attract urban professionals who value the convenience of city living.

Next, you need to create a compelling marketing campaign that highlights the property's unique features and benefits. This can include creating high-quality photos and videos that showcase the property's interior and exterior, creating a website that showcases the property and its amenities, and using social media and targeted advertising to reach potential buyers.

Another key aspect of luxury property marketing is building relationships with potential buyers and their agents. This can be done by hosting open houses and events, providing personalized tours of the property, and offering incentives for buyers who make an offer.

Finally, it is important to work with a team of experts who can help you navigate the complex world of luxury property marketing. This can include real estate agents, marketing specialists, and property management professionals who have experience working with high-end properties and know how to attract the right buyers.

In conclusion, luxury property marketing is a challenging but rewarding field that requires a unique set of skills and strategies. By identifying your target market, creating a compelling marketing campaign, building relationships with potential buyers, and working with a team of experts, you can maximize the ROI of your luxury property investment and achieve long-term success in the real estate industry.

Conclusion

Recap of the Book

The Complete Rental Property Course: From Finding Tenants to Maximizing ROI is a comprehensive guide for property investors. The book covers all aspects of property investment, from finding tenants to maximizing ROI.

In the first chapter, the book introduces the concept of property investment and explains why it is a great way to build wealth. The second chapter discusses how to find the right property to invest in, while the third chapter discusses the different financing options available to property investors.

In the fourth chapter, the book discusses the importance of property management and how to find the right property manager. The fifth chapter covers the different types of rental properties, including commercial and residential properties, as well as vacation rentals and short-term rentals.

The sixth chapter discusses real estate development and flipping. The book explains how to add value to a property through renovations and how to sell a property for a profit.

The seventh chapter covers luxury properties and how to invest in them. The book explains how to find luxury properties and how to market them to high-end tenants.

In the final chapter, the book discusses how to maximize ROI through effective property management. The book offers tips on how to keep tenants happy, how to maintain properties, and how to deal with common property management issues.

Overall, The Complete Rental Property Course is an essential guide for anyone interested in property investment. The book covers all aspects of property investment, from finding the right property to maximizing ROI. Whether you are a beginner or an experienced property investor, this book is a must-read.

Final Thoughts

Congratulations! You have completed The Complete Rental Property Course: From Finding Tenants to Maximizing ROI. We hope you have found this course to be helpful in your journey as a property investor.

As a final thought, we would like to emphasize the importance of continuous learning and improvement. The real estate market is constantly changing, and it is essential to stay up-to-date with the latest trends and best practices. Consider attending networking events, joining real estate investment groups, and reading industry publications to stay informed.

Additionally, always prioritize the needs of your tenants. Happy tenants are more likely to stay long-term and take care of your property. Regular maintenance and upgrades can also help maintain tenant satisfaction and increase the value of your property.

Finally, remember that real estate investing is a long-term game. Do not be discouraged by short- term setbacks or fluctuations in the market. Stay focused on your goals and continue to make smart decisions that will lead to long-term success.

Thank you for choosing The Complete Rental Property Course as your guide to real estate investing. We wish you the best of luck in your future endeavors!

Resources for property investors

As a property investor, finding resources to help you navigate the complex world of real estate investing can be crucial to your success. Whether you're just starting out or you're a seasoned pro, there are a variety of resources available to help you maximize your ROI and make informed decisions.

One of the best resources for property investors is a property course. These courses can provide you with a comprehensive understanding of real estate investing, including everything from finding tenants to maximizing your profits. Many property courses are available online, making it easy to fit them into your busy schedule.

Another valuable resource for property investors is a real estate investing course. These courses can teach you everything you need to know about investing in real estate, including how to find the right properties, how to finance your investments, and how to manage your properties. Real estate investing courses are typically available both online and in-person, so you can choose the format that works best for you.

If you're interested in managing your own rental properties, a property management course can be incredibly helpful. These courses can teach you everything from how to screen tenants to how to handle maintenance and repairs. You'll also learn how to create leases, handle legal issues, and manage your finances.

For those interested in investing in commercial properties, a commercial property course can be a valuable resource. These courses can teach you how to analyze potential investments, negotiate leases, and manage your properties. You'll also learn how to handle the unique challenges that come with commercial real estate investing.

If you're more interested in residential properties, a residential property course can provide you with the knowledge and skills you need to succeed. These courses can teach you how to find the right properties, screen tenants, and manage your properties for maximum profits.

For those interested in real estate development, a real estate development course can be a valuable resource. These courses can teach you everything from how to find the right properties to how to finance your projects and manage your team.

If you're interested in vacation or short-term rentals, a vacation rental course or short-term rental course can provide you with the knowledge you need to succeed in this growing market. These courses can teach you how to find the right properties, market your rentals, and manage your guests.

Finally, for those interested in real estate flipping or luxury properties, there are a variety of courses available that can provide you with the knowledge and skills you need to succeed in these niches. These courses can teach you everything from how to find the right properties to how to finance your investments and manage your properties for maximum profits.

In conclusion, whether you're just starting out or you're a seasoned pro, there are a variety of resources available to help you succeed as a property investor. By taking advantage of these resources, you can maximize your ROI and make informed decisions that will help you build your real estate portfolio and achieve your financial goals.

Call to action.

As a property investor, you have probably heard the phrase "Call to Action" before. It's a marketing term that refers to the specific action you want your potential tenants or buyers to take after they have seen or read your advertisement. In other words, it's a way to motivate your audience to take action and make a decision.

In the real estate industry, a call to action can be anything from filling out a contact form on your website, scheduling a property viewing, or even making an offer on a rental or commercial property. If you want to maximize your return on investment, it's crucial to have a strong call to action in all of your marketing efforts.

One of the best ways to create an effective call to action is to make it clear and concise. You want to make it easy for your potential tenants or buyers to understand what you want them to do and how to do it. Use action-oriented language that inspires them to take action. For example, "Schedule a viewing today" or "Apply now to secure your spot."

Another important factor in creating a strong call to action is to make it compelling. You want to give your audience a reason to take action. This can be anything from a limited time offer, a discount, or even the promise of a better lifestyle. Highlight the benefits they will receive by taking action, whether it's a better living experience, a profitable investment, or a luxurious vacation.

Lastly, make sure to include a sense of urgency in your call to action. This creates a sense of FOMO (fear of missing out) and motivates your audience to act quickly. Use phrases like "Limited time offer" or "Act now to secure your spot."

In conclusion, a strong call to action is essential for any property investor looking to maximize their return on investment. By making it clear, compelling, and urgent, you can motivate your audience to take action and make the decision to invest in your property.

www.ingramcontent.com/pod-product-compliance
Lightning Source LLC
Chambersburg PA
CBHW062352290526
45794CB00005B/2196